A Fish to Feed All Hunger

SANDRA ALCOSSER

A *Fish* to *Feed*

ALL HUNGER

University Press of Virginia

Charlottesville

THE UNIVERSITY PRESS OF VIRGINIA
Copyright © 1986 by Sandra Alcosser

First Published 1986

Library of Congress Cataloging-in-Publication Data

Alcosser, Sandra, 1944-
  A fish to feed all hunger.

  I. Title.
PS3551.L294F5 1986   811'.54   85-29619
ISBN 0-8139-1094-3

Printed in the United States of America

for my family
and for Philip

INTRODUCTION

"Poetry does not need to be defended, any more than air or food needs to be defended," Randall Jarrell told an audience at Harvard University nearly four decades ago. The conference at which he spoke was titled "The Defense of Poetry." "If we were in the habit of reading poets their obscurity would not matter; and, once we are out of the habit, their clarity does not help."

This collection of Sandra Alcosser's poems does not need an introduction. To paraphrase Theodore Roethke, she has served prehistory long and well. The women-speakers of these poems are accustomed to natural and preternatural threats, and to surviving alone with their allotment of hunger, lust, fear, and courage. The experience of strong emotions can give way to hallucinations, some frightening, others offering an odd com-fort, such as this passage from "In the Country":

> *Never have I felt*
> *unloved in the forest or lonely. Black cats*
> *stalk the cabin each night like gentlemen*
> *in tuxedos and I find them in first light*
>
> *spread out in the grasses and clover. Each one*
> *has his legs wound about his own body and his tail*
> *slung over his shoulder*
> *like the arm of an old friend.*

The narrative impulse in Alcosser's poetry is often marvel-ously complex, setting tone against content, as in "Ruddy Glow Against a Black Background." Two women, both rid of their men for different reasons, are roughing it on a ranch under the shadow of a volcano that has recently erupted. The upbeat tone belies the more sinister drift of the volcanic ash over everything.

Presented with a Monet-like sensuality, the misty pastels are, in fact, decaying. The women try to savor their imagined deaths by studying photographs of Pompeii. They want their bodies arranged just so. Meanwhile, they are preparing food and writing letters home to mother. The sinister and the lighthearted are hauntingly twined:

> Rica and I wear masks and silk blouses.
> Our cheeks are pumiced red. She has not looked
> this good since her husband left. Draped
> across the brass bed, she dozes. I watch blood
> blister under my hands. I cannot close my eyes.
> The guinea hens are dead. The horses stand
> in dust past their fetlocks. To touch flesh,
> I thread mushrooms, hang them from the mantel
> to dry. They make the room
> smell of decay.
>
> Each day is dusk and by dark we are mad.
> We build a fire, roast meat, dance outside
> on the white grass, raising clouds
> with our feet. Ash covers us
> like rice powder.

In a novel or a short story, the writer would take many pages to prepare for such radical shifts of tone. In this poem, however, the poet proceeds with the assumption that all these contrary levels coexist and are equally true. The volcano has provided a kind of solution to the problems both women have had with their men: it will bury them and they can take to their ashy graves a mock-romantic posture not tolerated in the difficult light of the late twentieth century.

There is a kind of knotted eroticism in many of these poems, one that is never fulfilled. Its potential is powerful and raw, even primitive, but as one partner is receptive, the other is crippled with a nameless anguish. Far from being a "war of the sexes," or a tragedy of the sexes, it is human need left to go begging by human pain. In one poem the speaker buys "a tomato-red brassiere," but it is a gesture that goes nowhere because her companion is grieving for "a bride who turned on the gas." In another poem, drunken ranchers taunt a woman school teacher late at night: "*Hey Kathy, we'll teach ya something.*" Presented without sentimentality, there is an implied compassion for their crude, hard lives. Earlier in the day the same teacher had accepted a love poem from a young prodigy named Damion because "he had to make his sweet verse for someone."

By turns tender, dark, sensuous, Sandra Alcosser's care for language is never far from center stage. In the opening lines of "Winning" the language is as deliberately loaded with menace as it is with sensuality, scoring the poem's central theme:

> *It is the temper of the razor*
> *as it skirts her anklebone,*
> *the amber globes of turtle oil.*
> *She lies deep on a green chaise,*
> *cotton between her toes, one leg*
> *raised, and flames each nail.*
> *More than one man has called*
> *her fingers perfect, the moons*
> *gibbous. In the dressing room*
> *the lingerie with hoya vining*
> *up the belly, the celery-colored*
> *cashmere dress and spiked heels.*
> *Tonight she will blur like gouache*
> *and tip forward.*

The diction is rich and appropriate. The effort that is made to please and receive compliments on her appearance might seem pathetic were it not for the contrasting scene depicted in the following stanza, an image from the woman's childhood of parents fighting "among the steak knives," paralleling the razor in the first line of the poem, a device Alcosser often employs to good effect, and never too obviously. One notices these foreshadowings and image-rhymes only on a third or fourth reading of a poem.

In other poems an image, seemingly not central to the poem, is actually doing serious subterranean work, as in this stanza from the long poem in sections, "The Journey":

It was spring. The trees were steaming.
The geese sleeping on our footpath were white
and still as ladles. Two moths had beaten
free their tight cocoons and lay confused and green
in the sun. I placed a branch nearby.
They crawled its length and threw back their heads
in a swoon, their wings flapping like fresh laundry.

Yes, it is an image of release, a gentle, even pretty image, but in the context of a poem whose narrative describes overwhelming adversity: a forced escape by boat from the immediate threat of a spring flood; the loss of that boat; a trek through waist-high snow; a broken limb; lengthy camping in a cave carved in the ice, and more. In the midst of this terror, the speaker of the poem dreams of aiding two newborn moths in their attempt at first flight. It is not just kind of her; it is an act of language and image making also that adds depth and texture to the poem. This poem is about duress and survival, but it is also about marriage, or a particular marriage. Finally forced to abandon his crippled wife in the ice cave in order to seek help, her husband "wore his body our whole married life like a shade," and has already butchered their dog for meat, places "a leaf of lichen on my lips for hunger, a ball of resin in my hands" before leaving. She finds, when she crawls out of the cave later, "everywhere my husband's confused tracks, his fragmented crosses." And, yet, clearly, she is relieved to have him gone:

> Staring into the blank sun, I am content
> to lie alone, to call back days so precise
> they are like the red patches of a kestrel
> in dark flight. The whole life of our cabin
> whirrs about me. The poppies of summer
> lay down their red skirts with the purple
> nightshade and clover.

Such tranquility for one with a broken limb abandoned in a cave of ice! And yet this is the magic of Sandra Alcosser when her many strengths combine to weave these rich, variegated narratives. Themes and subthemes tangle in the subconscious. They are not simple, but neither are they obscure.

A Fish to Feed All Hunger challenges and rewards those still in the habit of reading. Each moment seems to have its just emphasis. In our daily lives, we are performing a series of rites for one another. And Alcosser's sense of ritual is keen. She gives meaning when it is most needed.

JAMES TATE

ACKNOWLEDGMENTS

The author and publisher wish to thank the following magazines for permission to reprint certain poems:

The American Scholar for "Cry," first published by the United Chapters of Phi Beta Kappa. Copyright © 1983 by Sandra Alcosser.

Intro 12 for "A Fish to Feed All Hunger" and "The Divide" published by Associated Writing Programs, Norfolk, Virginia.

The New Yorker for "On the Veranda We Drink Gin and Tonic."

Nimrod for "Fox Fire" and "Nightjar." Reprinted with permission from *Nimrod*, international literary journal, published by the Arts and Humanities Council of Tulsa, Oklahoma, 27, no. 1 (Fall/Winter 1983).

The North American Review for "The Disposition of Hands," "In the Country," "The Journey," and "The Photographer Discovers America."

The Paris Review for "The Plant Ladies" and "Thief." First published in *the Paris Review* no. 71, Fall 1977.

Poetry for "Each Bone a Prayer," "The Entomologist's Landscape," "Learning the Gleaner's Song," and "Ruddy Glow Against a Black Background."

Poetry Now for "The Trap."

Portland Review for "Salamander" and "He Didn't Speak" (originally "The Photographer").

The Western Humanities Review for "The Banker's House," "First Flowers," and "The Sawyer's Wife," which first appeared in *The Western Humanities Review*, 39, no. 3 (Autumn 1985). Copyright © *The Western Humanities Review*.

Woman Poet—The South for "The Man in the Window" and "Winning." Reprinted by permission of the editor, Women-in-Literature, Inc.

Some of these poems were included in *Each Bone a Prayer*, a chapbook published by the Charles Street Press, Loyola College, Baltimore, Maryland.

Contents

I

II

III

A FISH TO FEED ALL HUNGER

I

To be a fish
In the waters.

Loveless and so lively!
Born before God was love,
Or life knew loving.
Beautifully beforehand with it all.

D. H. LAWRENCE

Fox Fire

Once I thought we would know everything,
that's what this was for, this fox fire,
this fragrant energy like nighthawks
screaming at dusk.

All winter I stalked elk that were down
from the mountain and starving.
I walked the low places where they galloped
through slush, the rocks where they wallowed
and pawed for new grasses, the tooth marks
on aspen, the mineral lick, the creek
where the water was roiled and milky.
I sweated through immovable snow
and fell down exhausted, but when I imagined
I'd stand in a thicket, my eyes glazed over,
my sharp breath, and know the cold
communion of elk, I was wrong.

Once I thought we were all gods
blessed and strutting this lovely planet.
The earth was a minor passing, like the path
down to our ditch for water, pretty
with serviceberry, but transient.
As a young girl I swung upside down
with other girls as we hung by our heels
from a jungle gym and contemplated heaven.
It was a silky place. I preferred
purgatory, like a dark café,
retrievers curled about the table legs
and the warm abraded doors.

At thirty-eight I'm still the babe
of my family. Once I thought they would teach me,

that even their last breath would be a key,
but now I see them drifting off from their easy chairs,
like a tribe leaving shore together, the television
blaring, their mouths sagged open, and when they
return for brief moments, they stare at me
as if I were a stranger.

All that I will ever know is right here
in the wash and till of my own ten acres.
Frost tonight and behind it the whole summer
so brief I can still see the bronco-faced calf
born to the bloody pasture and the brown trout
suspended in its first glittering insect hatch.
There will never be more than twilight, a valley
receding to glass. In this tiny paradise
of common flowers, the waist-high marigolds
blaze up like golden dowagers. Venus rises alone
and early to a cold black sky.

The Entomologist's Landscape

I go the circuit of my enclosure over and over again.
HENRI FABRE

He picks through the couch grass, here a black-eared
chat on its nest of blue eggs, and there in the red clay
a natterjack bathes its warty back. Henri crouches,
like a scarab in his yellow jacket, and waits.

His son, Little Paul, keeps a birdcage full of peacock
    moths,
all male. Downstairs a female slips off her pale cocoon
and stands shivering. Wet fur, maroon and white.
On her wings, enormous chestnut eyes. Henri carries her
in a bell jar from room to room. At night he and Little Paul
turn the suitors loose. They storm through the cypress
to the laboratory where they beat against
the white gauze bell.

When the bait is right, anything can find you.
I look across the river this morning where last I saw a grizzly
batting swollen salmon. A large man stands in a thicket
of raspberries, waving. He wears a tweed jacket
and patent leather boots. Perhaps it is the cottonwood bud
I smashed, dabbed behind my ear like bloody perfume.

Mother's gone off to Maine in search of a secret island.
She will gather lobster, rub their green bellies so they hum
as they enter boiling water. On the leeward side
she will meet a Rockefeller who mows his own
boulder-dense lawn. If I stay in one place too long,
grow my hair like a banner, and for the hummingbirds
hang out a red begonia, whose secret island will I be?

Other than the muscular man, only one person comes.
An old painter with a reducing lens, she grades
the landscape: the mountains are a bookcase
full of shale and lichen, the trapezoidal lightning,
the air that tastes of grape jam. By all standards,
she says, we are sublime.

I myself prefer small scenes. I would have liked Henri.
We could have spent the day together on our hands and knees,
year after year the same weed lot, studying the digger wasp
as she squeezed a wild bee to her breast, then turned
to lick honey from its gasping tongue.

The Divide

You could lose your soul in Bozeman, alone.
The topsoil is thick, the waitress is kind.
She will face you toward the fish tank.

When I am here I eat slowly, holding bread
in my hand as though it had a heartbeat.
Sometimes after a quarter liter of wine,
I take myself upstairs, stroke my own body.

Calamity Jane stayed in this hotel.
She sat in the Elkhorn and howled
at strangers. Half-crazed, she was carried
from a train to the Bozeman Poorhouse
days before she died.

I keep bags packed with that in mind: cress
and snails from my own stream, raw almonds,
a lover's sweaty shirt. And I hold
a clean image of the divide,

its hills cut like rare beef,
the two coyotes running before me,
full moon, their shadows in my skirts.

Nightjar

I work the whole day naked. Bees in dry knapweed,
aspen leaves jingling on their stems,
a forest of copper earrings. I slit zucchini,
nail the green skins to dry. Split kindling,
tweeze splinters from my wrists. Nothing
in daylight can harm me.

At five o'clock the flies are quiet;
blades come to life in the pine forest.
I gather the afternoon's tools, try them on—
hatchet, maul, rusty nails—lock them away.
Locked, I say to the door behind me.
Locked, the day is over.

In an hour the windows go black as mica.
Two lights flicker far down the road.
They move in a triangle, lips to fingers,
the cigarettes of hunters. One bends over
a dead animal, its throat curled open.
He carves out a broadhead of five blades
shaped for bear. It is a mistake,
a neighbor's goat, my own imagination,
a car moving deep in the valley.

I write my mother. She writes back.
*You are my rare bird. You must build blinds
and hide behind them.* Rare! I am a raven
that flaps about tasting carrion.
When I enter a room the air wrinkles
in my hands. I am not a savage.
I am not crazy, but come from a small town
where I was no beauty, dressed
in a windowless room, and still

the boy next door knew the scar
far down my spine.

It is midnight. I sit by a flame and listen.
Rats clack in the kitchen, traps raised
on their necks like pleated Elizabethan collars.
Truce. I want no more tools. Steel is awkward
in my hands. The moon, half-risen, illuminates
new clouds. They belly across the timberline
like dark cats.

I chose this cabin on the lip of a canyon
surrounded by fierce winds. In summer I live
on inky caps and blackberries. Now it is hunting
season. The men dress in bright coats and their boots
chant *meat, meat.* I pull my hair back like an old woman.
I cannot dance in my own cabin. I wear
a loose kimono and black bedroom slippers.
I do not move my hips or shoulders.

The Journey

1.

Hawk, he said
and ran to the window, happy
to see its black shape against the snow.
Months we'd been alone. The Christmas fir,
strung with candles and packets of pork fat,
lay abandoned beside our cabin,
the bald food of grackles.

But this was not melancholy weather,
our rooms thick with woodsmoke and lather.
It was my husband, his vacant hands.
Everything he owned—patched, dressed,
rewoven. Each dusk he split the kindling
to a thatch of perfect splinters, relit the fire
and began his long ritual of whiskey.

2.

One whole week the ice jammed and screamed
past our cabin. *Before the runoff,*
my husband said, *before the banks flood,*
we need to float the river to town.
The journey is dangerous in early spring, rain
to snow, then rain again and clawing
sleet, easy to lose the way.

We raced the braided channel through narrow canyons,
past gnarled cottonwoods and snow-silent meadows.
One grief-faced pileated woodpecker followed, tapping
his lonely branches. At dusk we beached the battered canoe

and climbed up to a ledge to sleep, my husband on one side,
and curled on the other, our silver dog, her greasy fur
reeking of pitch against my face.

All night the horizontal blizzard, snow sifting
over steep boulders and evergreens. By morning,
our heads rang like skillets with the cold, and below,
in the ragged waves, our boat torn loose. We stood
on a slice of rock, between overhanging forest
and river, a glass slope behind us, a waterfall
frozen silver, and nowhere to go but higher.

3.

Four miles we crashed through chest-high snow,
until I heard a bone crack and a limb snap from its socket.
I fell down sweating, my belly cramped and reeling.
We had reached a place where the drainage
widened out into flat field and high bare cirques.
I lay there whimpering while my husband
tramped a cross in the snow.

With gloved hands and branches, he shaped
a small cave. It took the whole day and most of the night.
I numbed to one place, unable to move, while the moon
rose and stars twirled as if they were on strings.
Afterwards we slid inside and rested there,
listening to each other's breath,
and I fell into a deep dreaming.

It was spring. The trees were steaming.
The geese sleeping on our footpath were white
and still as ladles. Two moths had beaten
free their tight cocoons and lay confused and green
in the sun. I placed a branch nearby.
They crawled its length and threw back their heads
in a swoon, their wings flapping like fresh laundry.

4.

By the blue light of the snow cave
the veins shone in my husband's hands
and under his eyes, as if he wore his body
our whole married life like a shade. As if he courted
diversity, waiting for its glittering pain.
He always loved the forest best, the mountains
for their storms, their clattering plates of talus.

I was the timid one, finding interest
in the day's repetitions, treasure in the high grass
near home. I could have lived my whole life
in the lupine meadow. I was that happy.
I understood the cutworm, the mole, the silver ponds
where the muskrat floated and dove all day
down into the corridors of shore weeds.

I remember how my husband whistled
when he butchered meat. *Come taste
the raw antelope,* he'd say. *It smells
so sweet.* Yesterday he brought me
the stiff, purple liver of our own dog,
and when I turned my head, he smeared
his hand across my face.

5.

This is the first silent morning, my husband
gone away. He placed a leaf of lichen on my lips
for hunger, a ball of resin in my hands.
How quickly we take on the oddest half of another,
how easily we let it go. I crawl out on the smooth ice
and everywhere my husband's confused tracks,
his fragmented crosses.

Staring into the blank sun, I am content
to lie alone, to call back days so precise
they are like the red patches of a kestrel
in dark flight. The whole life of our cabin
whirrs about me. The poppies of summer
lay down their red skirts with the purple
nightshade and clover.

Now I move my hands in the dense wet snow and once again
I am the angel of childhood. How little I've changed
the physical world, content to lie in its wild lap.
Deep in my chest I can hear my own lungs clacking,
hardly the sound of an angel, more like the wings
of a small bird ascending or the high-pitched
elegy of a cicada.

A Night on Goat Haunt

If you pack no meat, no perfume,
hang bells and heal all wounds,
there is a chance the grizzly
will let you sleep
         in his territory.

It is brilliant there, amethyst
and turquoise siltstone,
         sunset the colors
     of a salmon's belly
     grey around the edge.

The climb will make your eyes throb.
You will crave candles and whiskey,
but in the dark you cannot see
the shredded logs, the scat
of orange berries,
         only glaciers drifting closer
     by inches, blue-white water scalloped
     like moth wings.

Grizzlies walk the trail in green moonlight.
It's smoother, more silent. Dream-white
antelope float across your clearing,
tasting, marking footrocks.

The mountains by sunrise become a silver cradle.
You may sleep a few hours before departing.
Spiraling down with thirty pounds of tin and feathers
on your back, part of you will want
to remain. But as you cross the timberline
you'll see again mossy trees and strawberry blossoms.
         The glasslike fungus whose poison
     you could not name
will look delicious.

Tracks

There is a man under the wheel of my truck.
It want to pay him, drive off, but he is shivering.
His wife left him weeks ago. He has cut his thumb
and stained his coat. It is the first black ice
of October. I invite him home.

The creek outside my cabin tastes of sapphires and weeds.
A bald eagle feeds there twice a day on deer bones.
The stranger asks if I am afraid to live alone.

We drink rum and hot tea. He shows me photographs
of naked women lying in leaves, black and white slices
of buttocks, spine. I cannot identify one body.
Was this his wife? He never photographed her.
One breast was larger than the other.

And his father was a trapper. Do I know coyote?
It is all lust. Rub badger on leg irons
and bury the traps in moss. Wear soiled buckskin gloves.
The coyote cannot resist green musk. He'll dig down fast,
snap teeth on himself.

I remember what my mother told me about strange men.
When I was ten, one pulled up in a blue sedan
to ask directions. As I pointed west,
he unzipped his pants. My eyes were bad.
I saw nothing but his hand digging.

Fire to door and back again, I want this man to go.
He takes opals from his pocket, a rabbit's tail,
and drops them on my table. I rub fur against my face.
It smells of tar and sage. There is blood on the tip,
still wet.

I knew a woman in Port Angeles who kept wolves in
   cages.
Mornings she scraped deer from pavement, butchered
what was left. Her lawn was smeared maroon with liver.
When she looked at me, I too was flesh.

It is narrow in this valley. Evergreen. The animal pelts
are thick and shiny. He wants names, dens. Opals
for a trade. No bobcat here, I tell him, just poorbear
and beaver too mottled to skin. But a stranger
is a stranger. I will spend the winter
sweeping the hills with branches.

Ruddy Glow Against a Black Background

We float all afternoon, island to island.
Rica fishes. I hunt mushrooms
at the base of burned cottonwoods.
When we return to shore, we gather
our skirts into baskets
full of morels.

The fog is pearly. It pricks the lilacs
and makes our skin itch. By morning, tanagers
storm the windows. On the radio a man says
incandescent avalanche 200 mile west.
A cock crows all day, his throat
a dry volcano.

Five days' dust fills the creek like powdered milk.
The highway turns too slick to drive.
Flies dart through the cabin, high-pitched
as nighthawks. We kill them, first with newspaper,
then our thumbs, smearing their black
and yellow bodies.

Ranchers wrapped in wet hides a hundred years ago.
They built dikes to keep lava from the fields.
Rivers boiled around them and hot gases
twisted their water towers
into fantastic goblets.

Each day we make a list of what is missing:
garlic, oranges, black olives. I get drunk
on the last rum and tell Rica about my lover,
how he knelt down, put his arms around my hips,   17

kissed me hard on the belly. *Not now,*
I told him. *There will be time.*

The widow's son is the only man on this ranch.
He is moth-white. She says the air was dear
when he was born. He stands on the lawn
inhaling glass.

Rica and I wear masks and silk blouses.
Our cheeks are pumiced red. She has not looked
this good since her husband left. Draped
across the brass bed, she dozes. I watch blood
blister under my hands. I cannot close my eyes.
The guinea hens are dead. The horses stand
in dust past their fetlocks. To touch flesh,
I thread mushrooms, hang them from the mantel
to dry. They make the room
smell of decay.

Each day is dusk and by dark we are mad.
We build a fire, roast meat, dance outside
on the white grass. Ash covers us
like rice powder.

When the sky clears, there'll be years
of brilliant sunsets, but there's been no news
for days. We study photographs of Pompeii,
talk of how to arrange our bodies. Rica says
she will lie like the tanager in her red
and yellow shawl, one wing thrown open.
I write letters home, make jokes
for my mother, and dream the digger
who will come to take my bones
in his hands.

A Fish to Feed All Hunger

On the porch like night peelings,
bags of red hackles.
The fisherman is dressing,
capes of moose mane around him.
In his vise, he wraps the waist
of a minnow with chenille.

We wade downstream. I am barefoot.
The fisherman stands, thigh deep,
seining insects. Perhaps today
in this blizzard of cottonwood
it is the caddis that rises,
after a year in mud, from larva
to phoenix in four seconds.

The fisherman ties an imitator
of hare's mask and mallard breast.
He washes his hands in anisette,
then casts back, a false cast,
watching the insect's legs
break the water.

I line the creel with hay and mint
and lay in six pale trout. There is a pink
line that runs the length of a rainbow's
belly more delicate than an inner ear.
It makes the whole basket quiver.

The fisherman does not ask why I come.
I have neither rod nor permit.
But I see him watch me afternoons as I bend
to brush down my rooster-colored hair.
He understands a fish to feed all hunger.
And the lure is the same.   19

II

. . . everything that moves, loves and is afraid.

MADELINE DEFREES

The Disposition of Hands

like a swimmer in rapture in a wave
you wing your way blithely through boundless space.

BAUDELAIRE

1.

Because no one could find a cabin
in these green, nappy woods,
only the hummingbird, with its red
throat and sugar-fast wings,
reminds me of the city.

The dead blooms are picked
from the white impatiens
and see how they flourish.
The horses are groomed,
the carrots thinned.
It is simple pleasure, over
and over the same song
rehearsing grace, the first
raspberry of summer, bursting,
or the cry of a red tail, circling
as it dives on a dark vole
in the iridescent pasture.

2.

When the train curved and strained
against its full load of bodies,
David screamed, *please, I'm in pain.*
He'd followed me home again.
We stayed up all night in a diner

drinking coffee, David reciting
nursery rhymes.

It was wrong, the doctor said,
to follow an instinct.
We sat in his office the next morning,
the air like wilted lettuce.
David is your patient.

July, and David stands
by the clinic desk in a wool coat
and stocking cap. *I'll kill myself,*
he says, *if you don't kiss me right now.*

His arms held hawk-wide,
he soars twelve stories
from an iron balcony, crashing
through a sports car stalled in traffic.
David dead in the lap of a dying woman,
her mouth open, her hair
snapping like an orange flag.

3.

We save what we can. Mostly small things.
I scrape the seeds from the last tomato,
the sweetest honeydew, place them
on a saucer to dry. I remember the smell
of ripe melon when I was five, rising
from the shore as I floated
in the shallows.

My father lay on the sand, handsome
in white trunks, drinking beer
and telling jokes with my uncles.
And then he was running down the pier,
a spade raised in his hand.
He sliced the water so fast, I thought
he'd cracked my head open.
But it was a water moccasin
he slammed on the dock,
and with the blade, he chopped
its head free. I bobbed
in the water screaming.
When my father lifted me,
his whole body quivered.

Twenty years later, I stand
beside my father as he leaps
and swims in whiskey-deep slumber.
All night in the den, the lonely
song of a calculator, the ice
cracking in a glass.
I want to lift his head
and ask, *where does it hurt, Father?*
I toss a blanket over his shoulders instead.
If he woke we would
embarrass each other.

4.

Sometimes fire is my best friend.
I cup my hands and blow
into the hearth, not the blue flame
of news, but red ember,
the sound of fiber catching
and then the blaze.

My dog lies at the end of his rope
all day content to snap at flies,
curious about a field of squawking magpies,
but it's night now and not even deer
browsing in the garden can distract him.
He tips his throat to the moon,
and from the thick white ruff,
a long howling. It is the thrust
of fur, the sharp teeth behind
an ear, that he desires. Across the flat
of purple alder, an answer rises
and fills the night and soon the pack
has bound the acres of black valley
in its longing.

I stir in my sleep, shift my weight
closer to the fire. My spine
white hot, my skin about to pop open.
I long to turn and place my hands
into the flame.

5.
We go on reaching. Our hands,
those graceful wings, desire.

Above the orchard each night
a bright object spins through a blizzard
of meteorites, like a bottle
tossed to the sky, a spaceship,
its brief message inside. It will
play the sounds of earth—chain saw,
pitchpipe, the braying of humans—
to any life that finds it.

And for me, and for my family,
perhaps the grace of small deeds will suffice.
To remove the pine siskin from the cat's teeth,
to free the half-mad fox from its trap.
To carry tea and buttered crackers
to a dying aunt.

It is August. My family visits.
We lie out together in a bear grass meadow
sliding down to talus, ending in creekbed.
The Perseids streak overhead, their white bodies
leap to earth, a sheet of ice and dust ignited.

I watch my family—mother, father, husband—
their night clothes shivering in dawn wind,
their arms extended as though they too might
leap against the sky, and in that brief
hour before light, we are together, smiling,
sober, our limbs, our brains,
our one body glowing.

First Flowers

*Know me and know why some buds never
bloom.*
> PATIENT, PSYCHIATRIC CLINIC,
> NEW YORK CITY

Elizabeth is in the hospital
one week before spring.
In the park outside her window,
witch hazel blooms.

I cut magnolia branches for her,
sepals, thick angora. She pries
one open with her little finger.
The nectar is immature,
the scent bitter.

Days later, it snows again.
Leaves bang together. Flakes fine
as face powder stick to limbs.
I pass a shop with *Magnolia nigra*
in the window, petals
like violet bruises.

I imagine Elizabeth in her bed, counting
the buds as they freeze and fall off.
She thinks she alone knows life is delicate
and blackens easily.

I want to call her, say Elizabeth,
come down to the street and open
your fingers. The ground is warm.
Sap is rising. Spring in its desire
is green.

Salamander

My lover brought me
a salamander, its body
tender as cut flesh.

I put it in a glass bowl,
pond of daphnia and
mirror worms.

In the morning
we watch each other
the taste of salt
on our tongues.

I want to free
the salamander. Yet,
while it lives,
I cannot.
Clawless amphibian,
when I hold him
in my hands
I can feel the
print of skin
for days.

The Sawyer's Wife

We could go like your grandmother, over
the hogback and down the hill to the village
grocer for a loaf of bread, a sack of lentils
and the Sunday paper. Oh it's pleasant here.
Our boots are waxed. You've stacked the kindling.
There's plenty of wheat to grind and knead, hours
to watch it rise, but I want to go on foot today,
as she would, bored by her bright dishes,
the way eggs sat perfectly in their cups.
I need to check the flumes and weirs, the deer
tufts on barbed wire. I want to know
if the winter nests dismantle.

My husband is patient and charmed by a saw,
the sugary dust that falls in his boots,
the maul that tears red-blond fibers
as little white worms unravel; for him
the epic is home. The ants that leave
their trail markings in cedar are townsmen,
dark running matter, with or without heart.

Let's follow, like the trapper with a sweet
French name, this trail of peeled yellow pine.
See on this day, damp, how lichen plump
chartreuse and spongy on larch branches,
and our hair, wet with melting ice, fattens,
tangles in brambles. Only January
and listen, already the first shy
bargaining of birds.

They will be disappointed, my husband says,
we will all be disappointed, like the well
gone dry for lack of snow cover, the August
strawberry husking on its runner,
or the Chinaman who split the wall we walk—
rock that sparkled not with gold but wandering
glints of mica. It wasn't even his land,
but that of a lawyer who liked the word *ranch*,
the way cattle rumpled in his pasture, black
and white as newspaper. They celebrated together,
the fields picked clean, the pleasure of a wall,
and the rancher called him *Chinaman, Chinaman*,
as though he were his doll.

We'd come to look at nature, seeps and gorges
full of alder, red osier, blue grouse,
but this is the line between meadow and rock,
or call it failure. Good chicken weather.
Seed peas and apples when there's water.
Little more.

Here, Two Feather Sawmill with timber,
once enough to build a town, all plowed
in slash now, with rusting cans of antifreeze,
a shed of sawyers' gloves tossed down,
thousands of them rotting, open-palmed.

It's hard to live above the timberline
for man or woman. Rocks grinding all night,
sharp cries of animals we cannot name.
There was a ridgerunner behind our house,
a small man with no teeth who wrapped his feet
in dishrags. More than once, half frozen,

31

he broke into a summer cabin, opened
an abandoned tin of fish or jar
of rhubarb wine. Charmed sometimes by the valley's
false bowl of stars, he'd sneak down, pause
at a window to watch an old woman rocking,
doing recitation to herself. In the grocery
he'd finger the red cans, the ones with the face
of the laughing boy, and always before the town
went to sleep, he'd leave. Afraid of being beaten,
jailed, he'd climb back to the first swale,
bed under a ripped piece of tarp.

And aren't we like that, testing the world
in fits and starts, the bad distilled
and the good? We sit on the hill at dusk
to play out our long shadows. The snow
in the footpath twines two ways, up the mountain
into deep saddles and down through the hayfields.
It's five o'clock. The smell of carrots
and onions rises on an evening thermal,
and how seductive, the dark broth.

Climbing the Sapphires

I've climbed too high again
into the Sapphires, following
the track of whitetail, looking
for where the boughs arch, the cup
of red needles, a place to crouch
and watch the valley.

I've climbed until the footrocks split.
And you, higher up
on the other side of the same fin,
tell me I can walk perpendicular.

But this rotten bloodstone and pressed fern
keeps breaking in my fingers. I pull my joints
like venetian cord. I climb with a cat
that hung a hundred feet over our cabin
last winter. Wedged between two limbs,
it cried for days, then fell,
solid ice, onto our roof.

Every time I climb too high, I sweat and beat
the mountain. But you are there to talk me down.
I swing out, shift my weight, let your voice
believe me. I am graceful of this earth.

The One Who Binds the
Sheaves Last

1.

Noon. I sneak back through a thicket of chokecherries
to lie on your father's bed. Heat makes the white curtains fly.
In the kitchen your sister sings to herself. A lullaby.
Chicken spatters in three frypans. She's seventeen.
It is her first season.

A mile down the road you turn again over blond hills
and melancholy sinkholes, three thousand old acres.
The china closet crowds with dinosaur bones.
Choked in knotweed, the lake basin smells of sweat.
Three days and there is nothing left to explore
but a dump of snakes and chipped enamel cups.
I wait for you to come home.

2.

All those towns we worked together up and down the Missouri.
You wore the felt hat of an old man who died on tapioca.
I bought a tomato-red brassiere. Everywhere dark leafless
islands like tastebuds, waitresses who blotted
catfish and lettuce on the same towel.

I told you stories about Blue Earth, a world flush
with uncles and long-haired dogs. Perhaps you had no childhood,
or it began each time you ran away. The house you built
with hand-peeled logs. How you watched it burn.
And later in France, a bride who turned on the gas,
died washing dishes while you slept.

3.

Money, love, guts, there never was enough.
When you drove down from the hi-line holding yourself
like a Swede gone mad in winter, I made a place in my own bed,
rocked you like a mother, *Luscious*, you said,
and moved closer. That was not what I wanted.
Months I ground the berries you left behind into rough flour.
Your letters and dark wheat bread.

Best of friends, we say to each other as one of us packs
to leave again. You guide my finger north through haze
to hills called Sweetgrass, but you cannot escape.
You've promised to wait here for your father, years, reaping
horizons of dust. Clouds drag across your face
like white handkerchiefs. And the sky keeps pulling away.

Learning the Gleaner's Song

Sometimes at night I run down
the center line of the highway
screaming, and in this alkaline flat
no one hears me. Skin, touch, smell
all torn lose by wind. It sets
the black dogs barking and the kids
come drooling to school.

I am the teacher. I keep a cup
of soothing chamomile tea
and a drawer of exotic stories.
Each day I begin anew,
watering the sponge of gnats,
feeding the flytrap, pinching back
the fat impatiens. When the students
swarm in, still smelling of milk
and linen, sugary with sleep,
we begin with a lullaby.

> *I'll drink from the clear stream*
> *and hear the linnet's song*
> *and there I'll lie and dream*
> *the day along.*

Raising the shades, I focus
the light like a burning lens
on the face of the handsome
delinquents.

> See how Blake's Gay Spirit leaps
> welcoming the day, his head
> thrown back, his pastel feet
> in the jumping position?
> You can almost hear
> the bones crack.

After lunch we float together
in the dry yawl of afternoon.
Brenda stares out the window
as if the sky were her blue bedroom
with poodles and sombreros.
I can see her father
dragging heavy blades
across the salty fields, drawing
long, coffin-shaped furrows.
I want to erase my numerals,
the columns of wheat and chaff,
and chalk the slate
with bird wings.

Come spring, I will lose
these children like small quail
to the fields. Some will escape,
turn back toward town, the half
that's not abandoned—gas station,
grocery and tavern. At least one
will give his hands
to the sharp teeth
of a thresher.

And me, I'm the red brooding hen
my parents call clucky for her age.
On the playground today, Damion,
a young prodigy, gave me a love poem.
His head bent, a necklace of sow's teeth
clicking against his dark neck,
he had to make his sweet verse
for someone.

Thaw's coming, the time
each of us goes bobbing

in loneliness and error.
But this town never needed
a season for that. Last fall,
after harvest, I lay out
on the round loaves of hay
watching coyotes gather
by the dry lake basin.
At the tavern, tired ranchers
framed rattlesnake tails.
The wind carried their voices.
Hey Kathy, they yelled,
hey teacher.

Their truck pitched
as it crossed the tracks.
I scratched down
into the baled grasses and
watched them circle my house.
The refrigerator light flashed,
there was the sound of cans
popping, and four fathers sat down
on my porch stoop.

All night they stumbled
around the yard, about the rick
calling my name. *Hey Kathy,*
we'll teach ya something,
they said. Like dumb animals
they never once
lifted their heads.

In the Country

Once I was the world's ugly little girl,
dressed in green tulle, waving
like a rue anemone, I rode through
a parade in a black Mercedes.

Saturday nights while an entire city
paired off without me, I danced with a chicken
in the Chinese Arcade. Hours he spun in a glass cage
for his brief ration of grain.

How much easier, life in the country.
Warm coat, handsome socks and one stops
longing for company. The meadow crowds with blue
grouse, silver-leafed balsam root and below

a whole lush valley. Never have I felt
unloved in the forest or lonely. Black cats
stalk the cabin each night like gentlemen
in tuxedos and I find them in first light

spread out in the grasses and clover. Each one
has his legs wound about his own body and his tail
slung over his shoulder
like the arm of an old friend.

Cry

White legs and pink footpads, the black cat
loved me. It was summer, a perfect flush
of weeds and flowers. Mornings, he'd listen
for my kettle, the screen door snap, and he'd know
I'd come to breakfast in the asters. As I ate
my bowl of red berries, he'd burl and stretch
and claw about my hips.

One night as the cat and I watched the moon eclipse,
amidst the scuttling of bear and mice, there was a cry
from the forest, not seductive, but pained and wailing
like a siren. The next day the cat was gone. I'd heard
that even blackbirds broke veins in their throats
singing love songs. I stood by my window practicing,
trying to shape the feline song, to call him back.

My daughter was no different than a cat,
tapping the window glass over my bed,
crying at night till I rocked her frail ribs
against mine. Her hands on my breast,
dark curls sweated against her forehead,
tell me about the princess, she said, *the way
she slept in a blue dress, waiting.*

It was a month of heatstorms, lightning scratched
like Sanskrit across the valley. A boy came riding
our footpath. He wore black jeans, a sliver of green
malachite at his neck. The breathless afternoon,
the bees laid out on the red eyes of gaillardia.
Before she left my daughter cut off her long hair
and bleached it yellow.

There were years when I too turned from my mother's
cool white arms. First the pale boy, scarred
and silent, then my husband. We cleaned the ditches
together in spring, raking out the silt and dead branches.
He played a silver harmonica. A ring-boned pony
was what I had when we ran away. A field of salsify
and a black skillet.

Stretched out on the porch this noon, resting
my swollen legs, I'm tired of canning tomatoes,
the house thick with red steam and basil.
The bite of salt and vinegar, cucumbers
floating like green bathers in brine.
All that flesh I've tended gone to pulp.
All that mismatched tenderness.

One weed knows another and each animal has its own cry
and when it's right, it's easy. Easy as my husband
behind me now, holding open the black screen door.
He is drinking tea with honey and a halo of gnats
screams about his face. *Let's sneak down to the basement,*
he says, *where it's cool and dark.* He cracks a bead of ice
in his teeth and offers half to me.

III

In the case of passion flowers,
the trick is to stick them in the icebox.
They are so astonished at the various things
they find there, that they are afraid to shut.

WALLACE STEVENS

Winning

for Michele Taipale

It is the temper of the razor
as it skirts her anklebone,
the amber globes of turtle oil.
She lies deep on a green chaise,
cotton between her toes, one leg
raised, and flames each nail.
More than one man has called
her fingers perfect, the moons
gibbous. In the dressing room
the lingerie with hoya vining
up the belly, the celery-colored
cashmere dress and spiked heels.
Tonight she will blur like a gouache
and tip forward.

As a young girl, Saturday nights,
while her parents fought among the steak knives,
she sat on the edge of a bath, soaping up.
As their voices rose from the kitchen,
she hummed and dipped each limb in water,
till she'd shaved even the blond thistles
along her knuckles. Afterwards,
there were cool drinks.

So much smoothness. Sometimes she forgets
what she wants. Once a boa wrapped
about her as she watched the soap opera.
It was her brother's. He told her
it ate a young calf each month, alive.
She was nine, no bigger than a calf,
and each time she stood, its skin
tensed about her waist. The unnerving
temperature. She waited all afternoon
for her brother to come home and untangle
the snake. *Smooth,* she thought,
escape, and she smiled and kept
stroking its throat.

The Man in the Window

I've never seen his face. He keeps the shade
pulled so only a swale of his torso is visible.

Each morning in separate windows, we share
a meal of toast and eggs. It scares me

how our gestures are the same. Perhaps the heat
shapes us, like the leopard-skinned banana

curled against the fragrant peach.
Neighbors, they bruise each other.

But this man's hands are gentle. On the ledge
he waters a philodendron, his coral shirt

and trousers open. Carefully he peels back
a wind-broken leaf. He reminds me of my uncle

who wired chandeliers. When he retired
he bought a toupee and pasted it over his left ear

like a cheerful French beret. I thought it sad,
everyday his one bowl of stew on a hotplate,

his murphy bed, his blue mohair sofa. I'm older now,
I understand some men choose to live that way.

I sit in a friend's borrowed rooms, my arms spread wide
on her paisley shawl. Four succulent houseplants   46

and the company of a window. I am not that man.
This is not a dingy hotel room. The walls are white here,

my bright clothes are in order. I have letters
from friends to answer. Still, he is my neighbor.

I return from work to watch him.
At dusk when he pulls the shade I am waiting.

With his smooth hand he tosses black-seamed stockings
from the window, a white lace slip.

They inflate like silk pigeons, flap and twist
past Western Union, past sparrows in their vapor lamps,

then dive back to Chambers Street where they cling
to the pale linen shoulders of strangers.

I pour a glass of chablis and lean against
the fire escape. Across the alley of greasy fish,

the gyros and doughnuts,
above the whining doberman,

the broken-hearted siren, I cheer him on,
though there's no face in the window,

I raise my glass to the delicate haze
dancing in mustard-colored air.   47

Thief

enters the dream
like an octopus floating
in its own ink.

He takes everything:
ingots from the Philippines,
German pistols, chess queen,
your grandmother's diamond rings.

Maybe it's the sleepwalker
who mows your lawn,
eyes like sliced eggs,
or your wife's lover,
the neighbor's son.

It doesn't matter.
You knew he'd come.

His feet on the carpet
as though it were your skin.
You bleach the linen,
but you can't drown him.

He is your thief.
A kelp that needs its rock.
He holds you in sleep,
tentacles knotting.
He will leave you clean, clean.

Voodoo, Central Park

There is a pig's head hanging
from a sycamore in Harlem Meer,
a woman's earring knotted in human hair
placed within a circle of rice grains,
and as we follow Montayne's Rivulet
toward 104th Street we find a rabbit
with a knife in its breast.
Its rotting flesh smells like thick ink.
I ask the children to study an oak tree
with *Fistulina hepatica* growing at its base,
but they will not come near me.
The fungus is deep red and they swear
the tree is bleeding.

The Photographer Discovers America

In a gray cottage in Massachusetts
he chooses a blemished pear for breakfast
biting into its florid cheek.

Two ballerinas practice floor technique
on the hardwood boards, pulling their pink stiletto
bodies toward each other.

The photographer regards them casually, the way a dog
scratches an ear for pleasure, rolling his milky eyes
in their sockets.

First there was the visiting countess with spittle
on her chins. The nobles of France with lace hats
and furbelows. Loathsome Pomeranians.

He caught them all in his glass house, dissolved in silver
salt, paradise and its queer inventions—bicycles with white
wings rising slowly over grape hills in Provence.

And then, like Monet, he retired to his garden,
half blind among the winking anemones, the high-kicking
begonias, the faint scent of dying vegetation.

But America wanted to be discovered.
His host, with the fine disposition and red pigeon eyes,
invited special guests.

They assemble in graceful positions.
It is harvest season, the tables sag with glazed pies
and ruffed grouse, hills roll by like filmstrips.

Images float inverted on his frosted glass.
The photographer isn't certain what he's supposed to photograph.
Now, for instance, the host's daughter stands against

the weathered barn, a straw basket on her right arm.
Come see harvest, her posture says, my crops of kale
with its difficult head and maroon petticoat.

Her white uncalloused hand beckons. She doesn't care
that the photographer is blind, her flax dress has no texture
for him, her chin, no line. She wants him to point

his lens and snap. She doesn't mind that she is no more
than a smear of flesh in a famous man's eye, sweet smelling,
confused with the incessant drone of flies.

On the Veranda We Drink Gin and Tonic

The elephant ears
tired of hearing witty stories
twist flat on their stems.
The flashy camellias drop to the lawn
like abandoned prom dresses. In Baton Rouge,
the falling over begins. Unmindful,
we might dissolve like aspirin
in this moist night air.

If it's not the falling over,
it's the standing up.
The bartender keeps a battalion of rags
in white uniform. I've seen him
beat a peacock rug to bloody red.
Isn't that how the cubists began,
separating the white threads of canvas
into a field of broken glass?

Nature morte: shaping the guitar
from wood-grained paper,
laying it flat so that one might embrace
every side at once.
Three women lean on their elbows
like collapsing tripods
and see how their malaise fractures
into radiant blue prisms?

With a moment's stay against geometry
this landscape could turn suddenly impolite.
We might break each other open
like the clear pink coat of a shrimp.
Perhaps we'd become friends,
the way cartoonists drew Frankenstein's scars
with zippers, as if anyone could
enter his curious skin.

The Banker's House

This is the house we wanted, the wainscot,
the plate rails, the light split
through pin oaks. Buttoned against summer
since the banker died, see how the nests
go untorched in the eaves, honey
dripping all day down leaded windows,
and the black tornado of bees?

I sit on the lawn eating cottage cheese
and ripe tomatoes. Behind a curtain
in the next house, the red curve
of a neighbor's shoulder advances, retreats.
Fascinated, she drums her nails on a sill,
studies me as if I were a delicate mold
growing on jelly.

From the post office, old men follow
me home, their teeth out. They finger
the marble basins, the blue hydrangea
wallpaper and ornate silver knobs.
The banker, they say, *had square posture.*
He was very brave. He smoked a bear
out of its cave in Montana, shot it in the neck.
It lay here on this parquet floor for years,
strafed by one shoe then another. It hangs
upside down in the basement now, infested
with fleas.

He never gave anything away. Campaign buttons
and chamber pots, we are cleaning
his death out. We are spraying the fissures
where his family lives. Evenings, we take off
our scouring gloves, lay them on their backs

like tired bathers. Our friends come to visit.
We drink young gamay wines.

It is morning and I am alone.
Behind me on the back stairs, slippers
are snapping. It is the banker again.
He shuffles through the kitchen in a plaid robe
he picked from the trash. *Bring me a bowl of gruel,*
he says, *with a sprinkling of nutmeg.*
And close the windows. There is a light
October wind. The odor of mice
rises from the storm cellar, and as I move
from room to room, his curtains lift,
twist about like yellow gauze wrappings.

Winter in Iowa

Now we will come inside, my dogs,
the twelve rich widows next door
and I.

The farmers have left for Paris
or Long Beach, but we will not
try to escape.

The pond is set with leg traps.
Pheasant breasts are salting,
scattering lice in basements.

I will sit in my nightgown
in this cheesy house till noon.
On the porch, one last hot
pepper plant blooms.

It doesn't know we've given up water,
the trees, the old bouquet of ladies and I,
not so much to die, but to come
to ourselves inside.

The dogs, on the other hand, are too young.
Half-wolf and howling this morning
in all my rooms, they are afraid of snow,
it is a trick, a yard of teeth.
In their hunger for red, they have eaten
the rugs, the mohair sofa, and if I sleep
too long, they gnaw my wrists
like chicken necks.

The Plant Ladies

I was sent to my room to think things over
So I sat with a white dog
On the ledge
Twenty stories high in golden haze
Concrete belfry
Breathing black oxides from the East River Drive
Watching the turd-eating seagulls dive.

Periodically a maroon Cadillac passed
Under my window and tooted
It's Now or Never into the wind.

Friend Dorothy on the eleventh floor
Had all the best shrinks
Gurus
Five brilliant husbands
And a consciousness-raising group.
She never got solved either.
Stacked together in a dead-faced totem
We stared west at the Statue of Liberty,
There was no choice.

But Burpee Seeds saved us.

Nursery stock
Like broken nerve endings
Bugged
Rotted.
We pick, pick, pick, deadhead
Loosen the earth, massage the roots
Whisper
Play Bach flute sonatas and
They survive.
We become the plant ladies.

Our souls spore-born
Heart-shaped gametophytes
Descend
Lie like liverworts
On sweet sour soil.
Bodies left behind in a room of wallflowers.
Baby tears.
No one notices.

Fern women
Hairy creepers
With untouchable
Heads like sores
Up from swamps, thick and malarial
We possess seed, sex, fruit.

Wind gives us rebirth
Sweet everlasting, virgin's-bower
Corn cockle
Sunflower
Moonflower fanned by ten-inch
Tongue of hawkmoth
Darwin's dream
Bush bean
Columbine
Silver queen.

And Dorothy calls herself Iris.

Detectives on our trail
But we do not fit the description.
Scabs, cankers, slugs
Suck, pierce, chew
Sow bugs
Maggots
Crotch weavers
Coddling caterpillars.
We will not be eaten or taken alive.

He Didn't Speak

But when they met,
he gave her a photograph

of lady's slipper, its lips
lavender and drooping.

She married him and the photographs
turned red, red as salvia and iron oxide.

Eight years later, ears ringing,
she left. He didn't write,

but sent instead, photographs:
orchards of breasts and black fungus,

racks of Chinese vegetables,
images grown more brilliant each year

as lichen do when they eat stone, dissolving
the color within, breaking it to pieces.

The Trap

For Christmas I gave him a jar
of three-fruit marmalade made
with barley water. He spooned it
after dinner, admiring the color
of pore and rind.

Once again we slept together
back to back, husband and wife.
All night I wanted to turn, open
my arms, but I remembered last summer,
alone in the new place, how I watched
a mouse lick soft brie from a trap
I'd set. The spring was rusty. It took
a long time to snap.

Each Bone a Prayer

Your letters arrive frail from Nepal.
Stamps of antelope and monkey dancers, laughing
though they have not seen fruit in days.

Outside Manang women watch you.
A nomad wearing dangling jade
waves you into her tent. From her hands
you take a bowl of yak milk. Delicious.
You would remain, but the sky
already rots with water.

Crossing the pass at Thorong La, your brain
begins to swell. You sleep in the arms
of a sherpa who feeds you opium, picks
leeches from your body. You would die,
but the rain is too lonely.

In the valley his family touches your chest,
the curly black hair, and says *fine. Very fine.*
You swim with buffalo in the river. A child
washes her mother there. She pulls off a piece
of the dead woman's shoulder and shares it
with her father.

You are wearing white robes when I see you.
I finger a gift of Himalayan fossils
and cannot name one bone. This was my home too,

now every room smells of woodsmoke. Rags blessed
by the Dalai Lama hang at the windows, yellow muslin
and ink fading as they fly prayers
onto a humid East River night.

In Nepal, you tell me, love is easy,
all wheels are spun clockwise, and the dead
are buried comfortably in the walls
of their own homes.

ABOUT THE SERIES

Since 1984 Old Dominion University has sponsored publica-
tion of the winning manuscript in the annual Associated Writ-
ing Programs Award Series in Poetry, an open competition
for book-length manuscripts. Established in 1974, the award
carries a $1,000 honorarium and publication of the manuscript
by the University Press of Virginia under a cooperative agree-
ment between AWP, ODU, and the Press. Virginia Common-
wealth University sponsored the publication from 1974 to
1982 under a similar agreement.

Manuscripts are received by AWP and are divided among
judges who are members of the AWP Board of Directors, all of
whom are nationally recognized poets. Finalists are selected
and the manuscripts are submitted to a panel of poets serving
as final judge in the series. Final judges for the series have
included Richard Eberhart, Elizabeth Bishop, Robert Penn
Warren, Donald Justice, Maxine Kumin, William Meredith,
W. D. Snodgrass, and John Frederick Nims. James Tate se-
lected *A Fish to Feed All Hunger* as the first-place winner in
the 1984 AWP Award Series.

For further information and guidelines for submission write:
The Associated Writing Programs, Old Dominion University,
Norfolk, VA 23508.

ABOUT THE AUTHOR

Sandra Alcosser grew up in Indiana and now lives in the Bitter-root Mountains of western Montana. She was educated at Lake Forest Academy, Purdue University, and received an MFA from the University of Montana where she studied with Rich-ard Hugo. Ms. Alcosser's poems have appeared in *The New Yorker, The North American Review, The Paris Review, Poetry* and many other magazines and anthologies. She is the recipient of *The American Scholar's* Mary Elinore Smith Poetry Prize, a Bread Loaf Scholarship, and a *Mademoiselle Magazine* Guest Editorship in Fiction and Poetry. Formerly the Director of Poets-in-the Park, Central Park, she has also served as a Visiting Artist for the Montana and Iowa Arts Councils. Currently she is an NEA Fellow on leave from Louisiana State University in Baton Rouge. In January 1986 she will join the creative writing faculty of San Diego State University as an Associate Professor of English.

*These titles are the first selections in
the Associated Writing Programs annual
Award Series in Poetry*

Sponsored by Virginia Commonwealth University

MOVING OUT
        David Walker
THE VENTRILOQUIST
        Robert Huff
RITES OF STRANGERS
        Phyllis Janowitz
JAMES COOK IN SEARCH OF TERRA INCOGNITA
        Jeanne Larsen
FOLLOWING GRAVITY
        James Applewhite
THE HOURS OF MORNING
        William Carpenter
DAYS OFF
        Paul Nelson
LEVERAGE
        Jonathan Holden

Sponsored by Old Dominion University

FLIGHT PATTERNS
        Lisa Ress
A FISH TO FEED ALL HUNGER
        Sandra Alcosser

University Press of Virginia   *Charlottesville*